P9-CRM-077

ONE DAD, ONLY ONE. FOR BILL CLEMENTS—A.C.
FOR JOHN FOOTE—L.S.J.

Text copyright © 1992 by Andrew Clements.
Illustrations copyright © 1992 by Lonni Sue Johnson.
Published by Picture Book Studio Ltd., Saxonville, Massachusetts.
Distributed in the United States by Simon & Schuster.
Distributed in Canada by Vanwell Publishing, St. Catharines, Ontario.
All rights reserved. Printed in Hong Kong.

Library of Congress Cataloging-in-Publication Data
Clements, Andrew, 1949-
Mother Earth's counting book / by Andrew Clements ; illustrated by Lonni Sue Johnson.
p. cm.
Summary: Enumerates some of the features of the planet Earth, including its climate zones,
oceans, and deserts, going from one up to ten and then back down to one again.
ISBN 0-88708-138-X : $15.95
1. Counting—Juvenile literature. 2. Earth—Juvenile literature.
[1. Earth. 2. Counting.]
I. Johnson, L. S. (Lonni Sue), ill. II. Title.
QA113.C54   1990
513.2—dc20[E]   90-7343
CIP
AC

Ask your bookseller for these other Picture Book Studio books written by Andrew Clements:
Big Al illustrated by Yoshi
Noah & the Ark & the Animals illustrated by Ivan Gantschev
Santa's Secret Helper illustrated by Debrah Santini
Billy and the Bad Teacher illustrated by Elivia Savadier
And this book illustrated by Lonni Sue Johnson:
The Story of Z by Jeanne Modesitt

MOTHER EARTH'S COUNTING BOOK

ANDREW CLEMENTS

LONNI SUE JOHNSON

PICTURE BOOK STUDIO

1 earth

only 1

2 poles

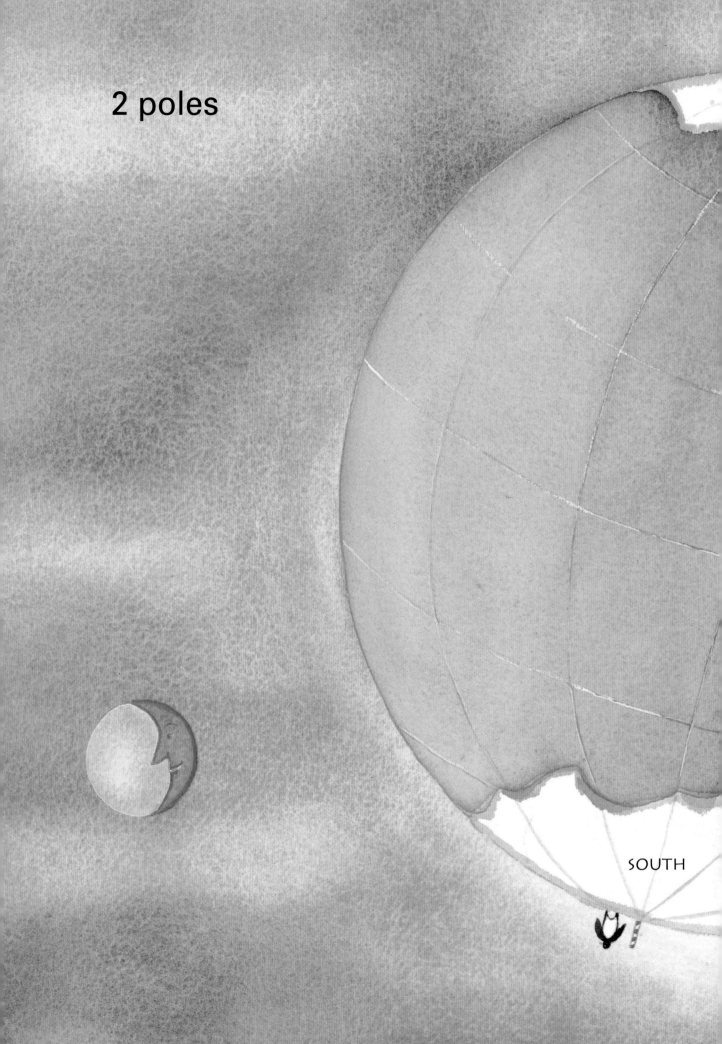

SOUTH

NORTH

only 2

3 climate zones

POLAR

TEMPERATE

TROPICAL

only 3

4 oceans

INDIAN

ARCTIC

PACIFIC

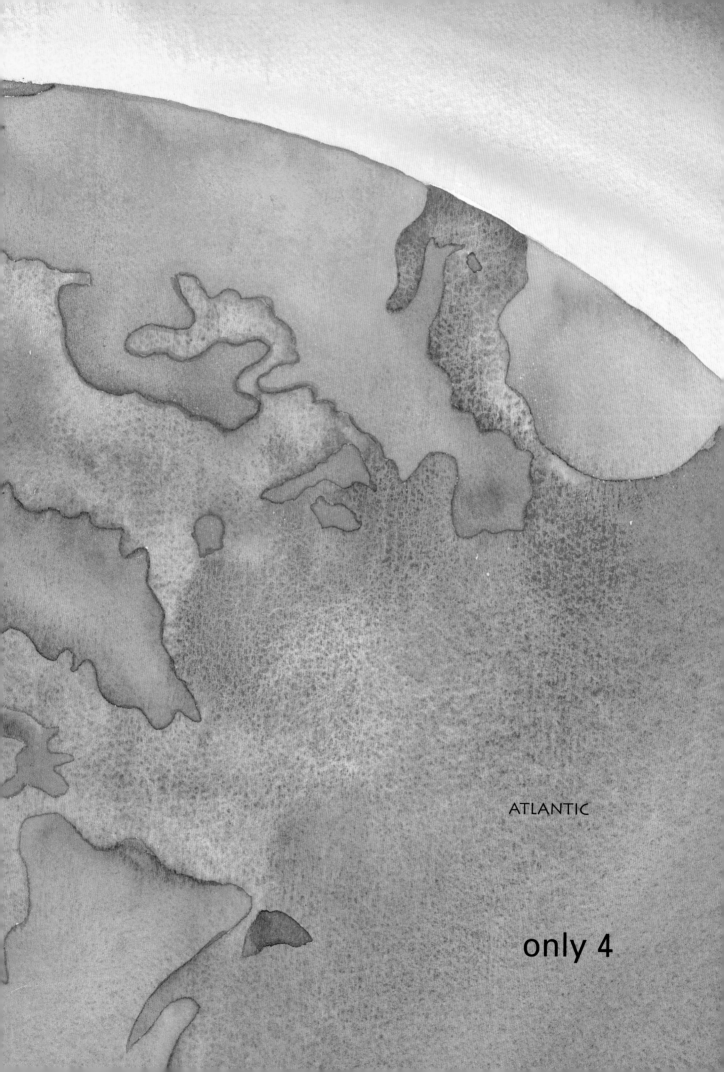

ATLANTIC

only 4

5 islands

BAFFIN

TAHITI

MADAGASCAR

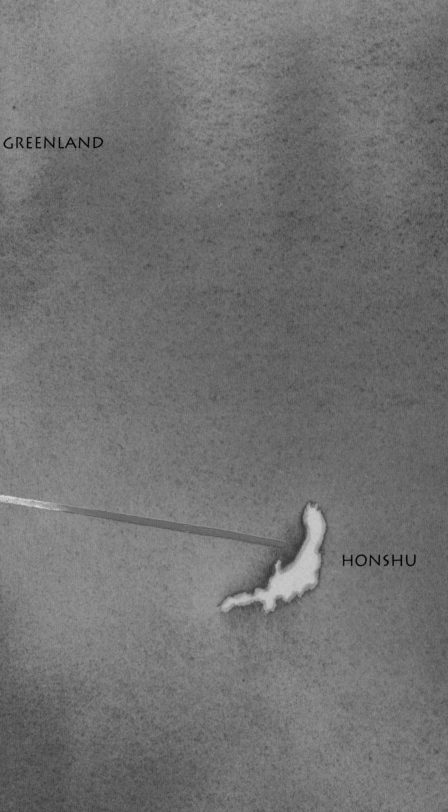

GREENLAND

HONSHU

and many more

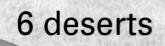

6 deserts

GOBI

CHIHUAHUAN

GREAT SANDY

SAHARA

ATACAMA

KALAHARI

and many more

7 continents

NORTH AMERICA

SOUTH AMERICA

AUSTRALIA

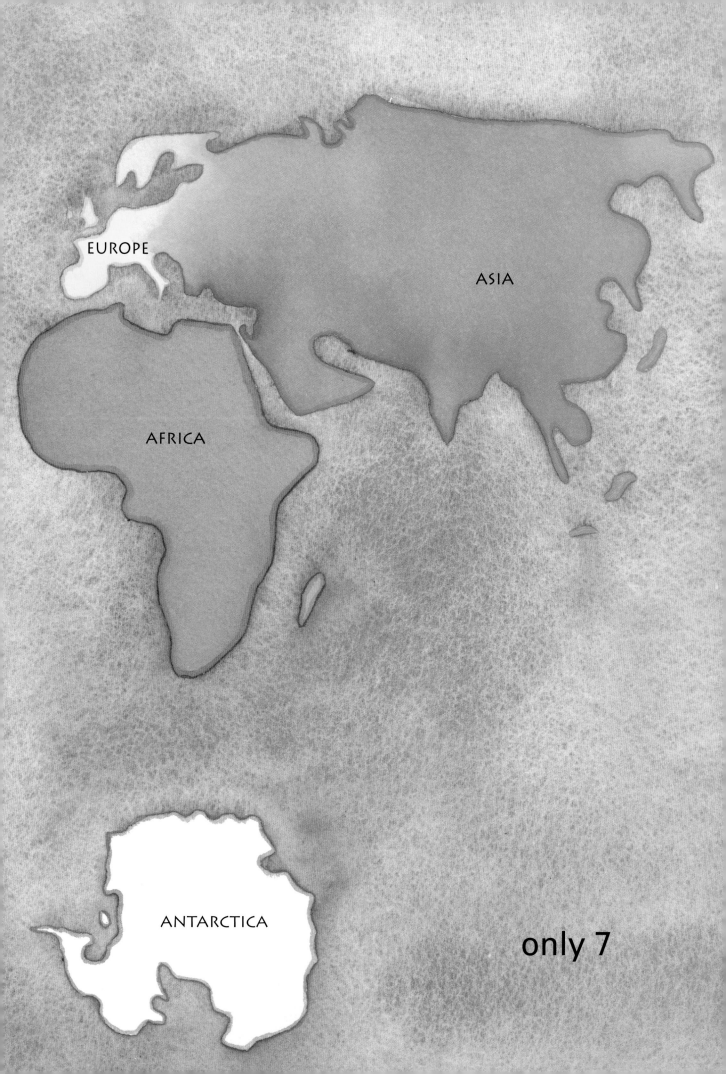

EUROPE

ASIA

AFRICA

ANTARCTICA

only 7

8 birds

WREN

DUCK

PENGUIN

FLAMINGO

R0080120806

HAWK

OWL

GULL

HUMMINGBIRD

and many more

9 mammals

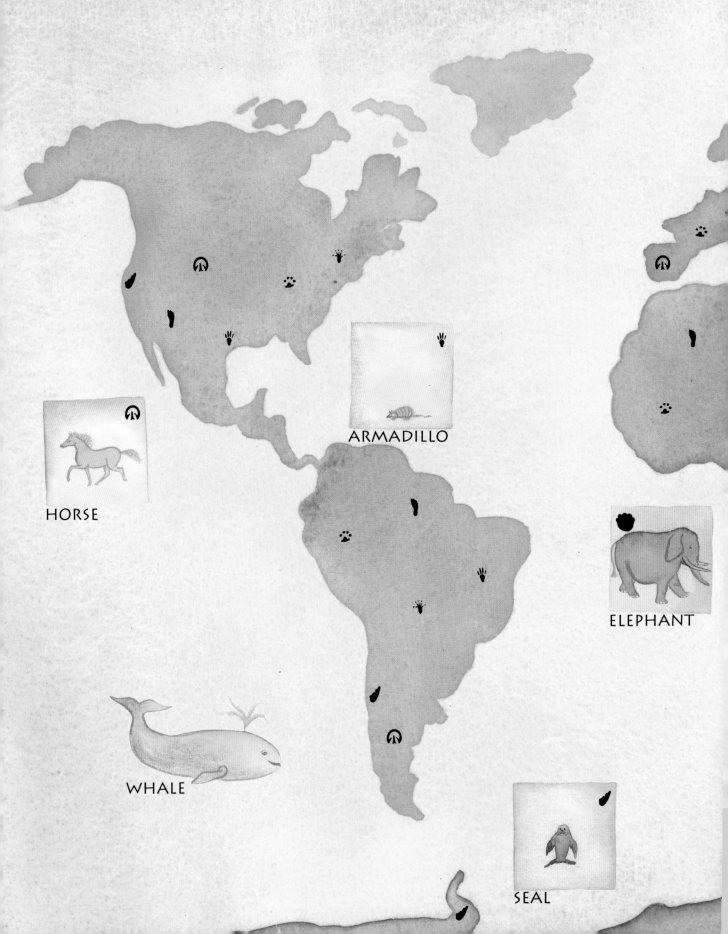

HORSE

ARMADILLO

ELEPHANT

WHALE

SEAL

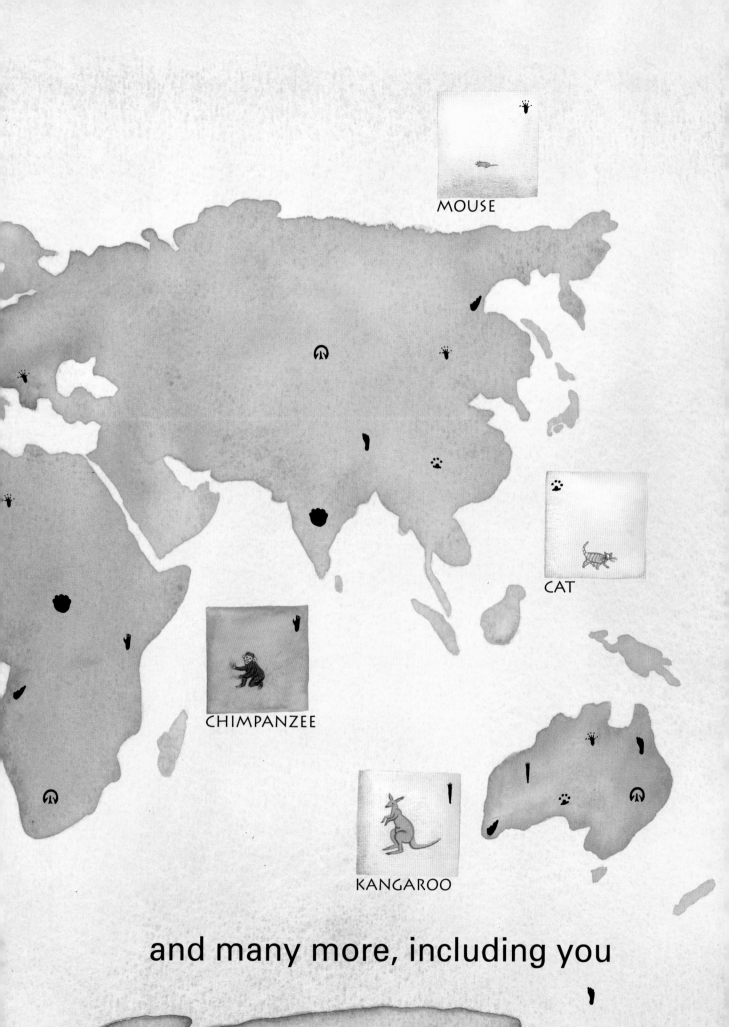

MOUSE

CAT

CHIMPANZEE

KANGAROO

and many more, including you

10 fishes

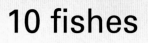

SWORDFISH

GOLDFISH

TROUT

CATFISH

SEA HORSE

PIRANHA

SHARK

SALMON

EEL

TUNA

and many more

10 plants

RICE

FERN

KELP

WHEAT

FIR
TREE

KELP

DANDELION

APPLE
TREE

CHRYSANTHEMUM

WATER
LILY

and many more

SAGE

9 peoples

MELANESIAN

MICRONESIAN

INDIC

EUROPEAN

ASIATIC

AFRICAN

AUSTRALIAN

POLYNESIAN

AMERICAN
INDIAN

only 9

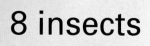

CICADA

GRASSHOPPER

LADYBUG

ANT

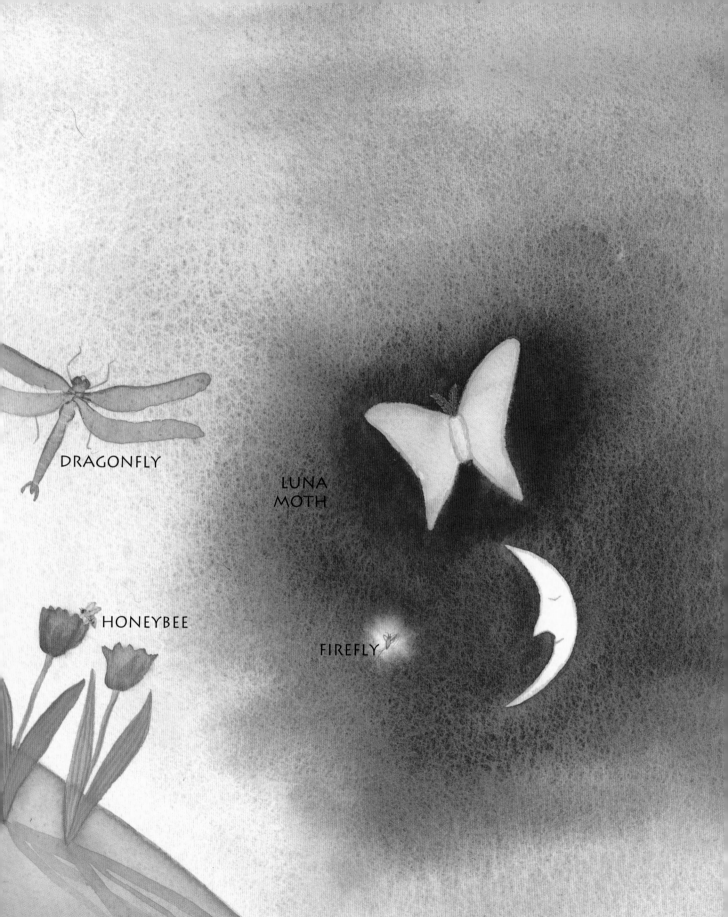

DRAGONFLY

LUNA
MOTH

HONEYBEE

FIREFLY

and many more

NORTH

MEDITERRANEAN

RED

and many more

6 mountains

MONT BLANC

KOSCIUSKO

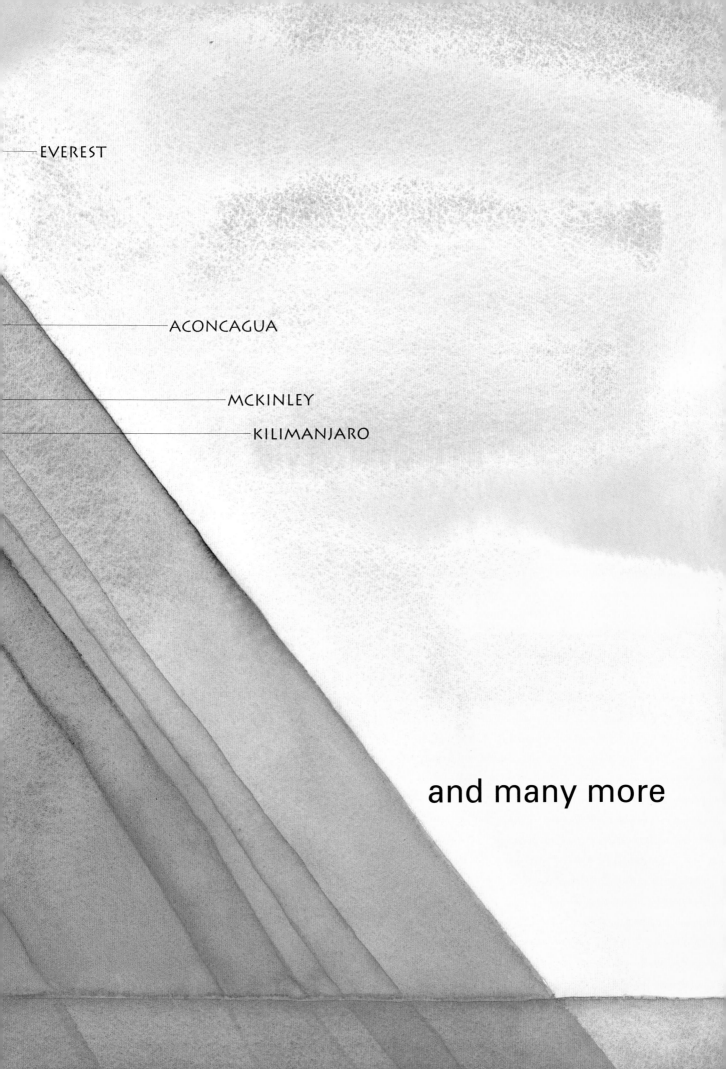

EVEREST

ACONCAGUA

MCKINLEY

KILIMANJARO

and many more

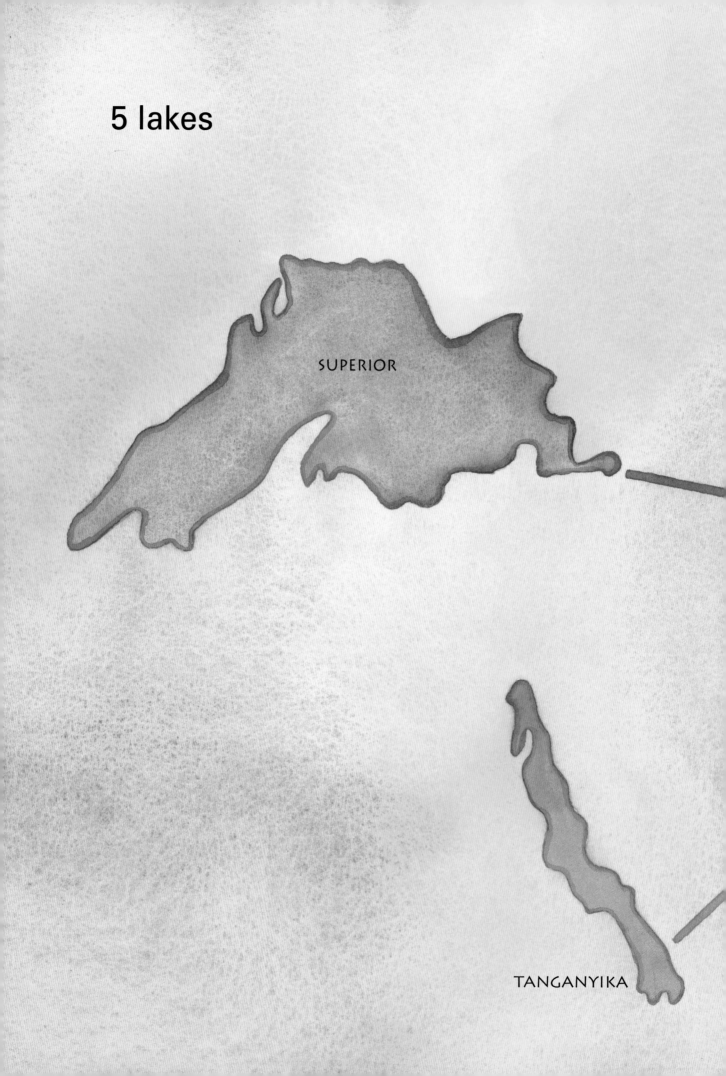

5 lakes

SUPERIOR

TANGANYIKA

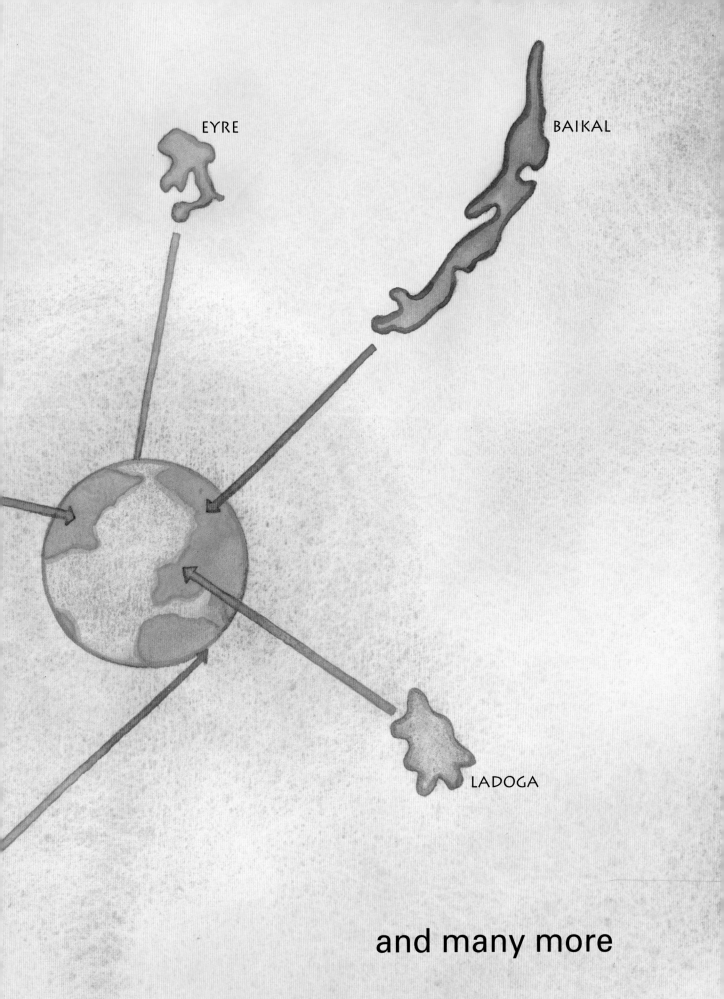

EYRE

BAIKAL

LADOGA

and many more

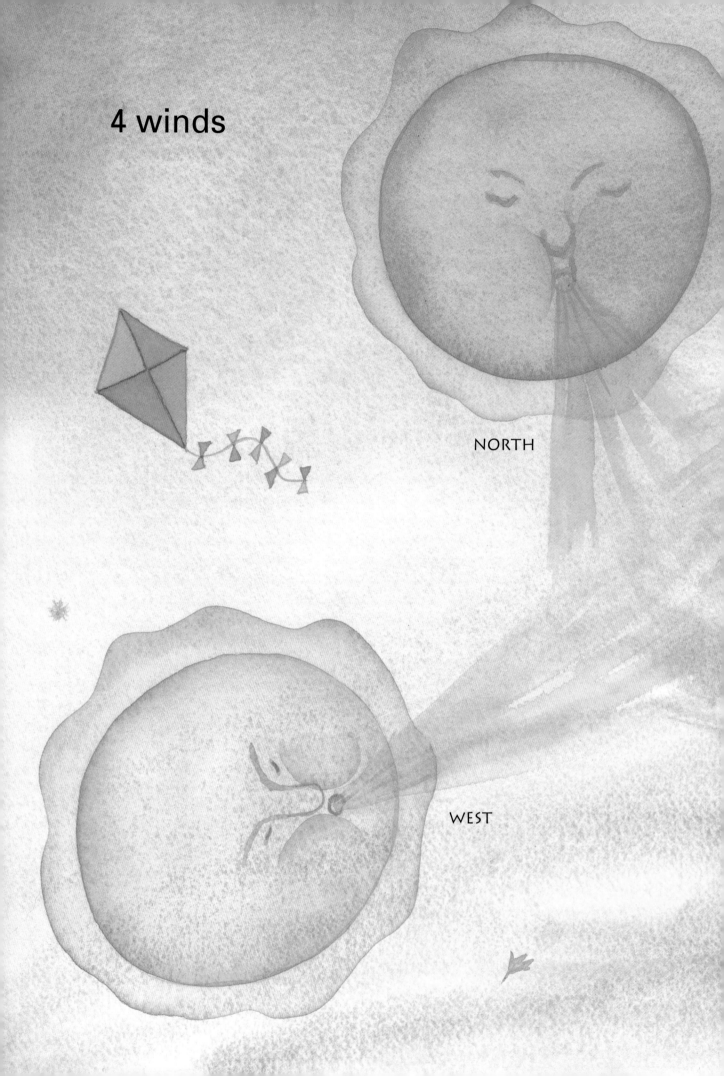

4 winds

NORTH

WEST

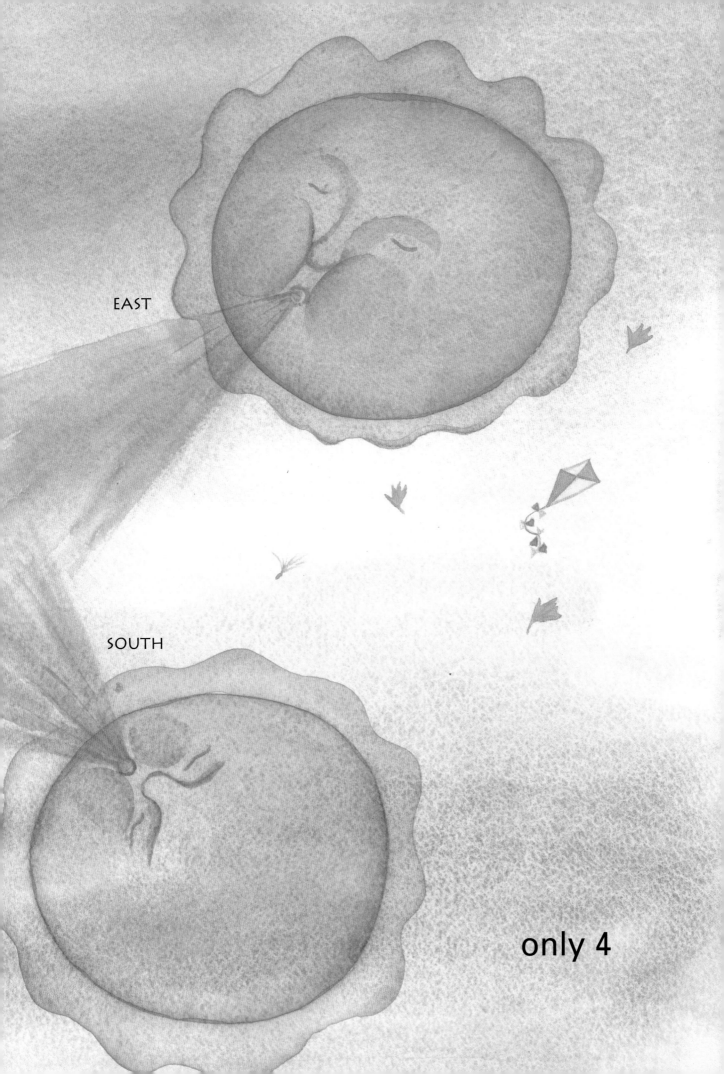

EAST

SOUTH

only 4

3 rivers

MISSISSIPPI

AMAZON

NILE

and many more

2 hemispheres

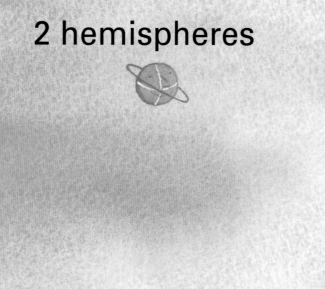

WESTERN

EASTERN

SOUTHERN

and 2 more

1 earth

only 1

Mother Earth's Counting Book is a short book which is designed to make you think about the whole Earth all at once. It explores our planet both as an object with many different features, and as a place that is home to many different life forms. Excluding the Earth itself, there are 108 different things named in the book, and that seems like a lot—until you realize how many other things are not mentioned. This book is possible only because most things are left out.

1 earth only 1	The beginning...

2 poles	The rotating Earth turns on these two points:
NORTH	Below the icecap at the north pole is the Arctic Ocean.
SOUTH	Below the icecap at the south pole there is land—Antarctica.
only 2	

3 climate zones	As the Earth tilts toward and away from the sun, the seasons change:
POLAR	dark and frigid in winter, bright but still cold all summer
TEMPERATE	cold or cool in winter, warm or hot in summer
TROPICAL	warm, or hot and steamy all year long
only 3	

4 oceans	From largest to smallest area:
PACIFIC	64,000,000 square miles
ATLANTIC	33,000,000 square miles
INDIAN	28,000,000 square miles
ARCTIC	5,000,000 square miles
only 4	

5 islands	One in each ocean, plus an extra one in the wide Pacific:
BAFFIN	Arctic Ocean; polar zone
HONSHU	Pacific Ocean; largest of Japanese islands; temperate zone
TAHITI	Pacific Ocean; example of the tropical island paradise
MADAGASCAR	Indian Ocean; Earth's fourth largest; environmental damage hotspot
GREENLAND	Atlantic Ocean; Earth's largest island; unspoiled environment
and many more	

6 deserts	These are some of Earth's most significant dry spots:
SAHARA	northern Africa; largest desert in the world—and growing
KALAHARI	southern Africa's largest
CHIHUAHUAN	largest in North America
GOBI	largest in Asia
GREAT SANDY	largest in Australia
ATACAMA	only large desert in South America—also the driest spot on Earth
and many more	

7 continents From largest to smallest area:
ASIA 17,000,000 square miles
AFRICA 11,500,000 square miles
NORTH AMERICA 9,000,000 square miles
SOUTH AMERICA 7,000,000 square miles
ANTARCTICA 5,500,000 square miles
EUROPE 4,000,000 square miles
AUSTRALIA 3,000,000 square miles
only 7

8 birds From an enormous variety of sizes, characteristics, ranges, habits:
GULL sea bird; omnipresent
OWL nighttime hunter
FLAMINGO tropical wader
HUMMINGBIRD tiny pollinator
WREN songbird extraordinaire
HAWK daytime hunter
PENGUIN Antarctica's one-of-a-kind swimming wonderbird
DUCK world traveler; wild and domesticated
and many more

9 mammals All except the cat and the seal are from different orders:
CHIMPANZEE jungle dweller; primate (same order as mankind)
WHALE sea dweller; cetacean (from Greek word *kete*—sea monster!)
CAT land dweller; carnivore (meat eater)
ELEPHANT largest land mammal; endangered proboscidean (having a big nose)
MOUSE all climates; everywhere but Antarctica; rodent—most numerous mammals
SEAL lives at each continent's shore; carnivore (a pinniped—"foot-like-a-wing")
KANGAROO like many, unique to Australia; a diprodontal (two front teeth) marsupial
HORSE everywhere but Antarctica; a large perissodactyl (odd number of toes)
ARMADILLO found in North and South America; edentate (toothless)
and many more
including you

10 fishes Ten fishes, because so much of Earth is covered by water:
TUNA salt sea fish that travels in schools
TROUT found in oceans, lakes, rivers, and brooks
EEL fresh and saltwater fish with a distinctive body type
CATFISH river fish; bottom dweller; world ranging, but largely tropical
GOLDFISH fresh water fish; revered in Japan and Asia for beauty and long life
SHARK ancient, successful species (whale shark is Earth's largest fish—over 50 feet)
SALMON sea and river dweller; mighty upstream swimmer; environmentally at-risk
SWORDFISH one of the ocean's most dramatic creatures
PIRANHA small South American river fish; famous, but not really so deadly
SEA HORSE ocean creature; shows how unusual, charming and graceful a fish can be
and many more

10 plants

Ten plants, for their beauty, and for their importance to all life on Earth:

CHRYSANTHEMUM	temperate area flower
APPLE TREE	temperate fruit tree
FERN	temperate and tropical forest floor dweller
SAGE	hardy desert dweller
KELP	floating salt water plant in all oceans
DANDELION	temperate zone; weed to some, salad to others
WHEAT	temperate zone's most basic food crop
RICE	tropical zone's most basic food crop
WATER LILY	temperate and tropical fresh water plant; rooted to the bottom
FIR TREE	temperate zone conifer (with seed cones); an evergreen

and many more

9 peoples

The geographical races of mankind, defined by where they originated:

AFRICAN	originating in Africa below the Sahara desert
AMERICAN INDIAN	native peoples of North and South America, akin to Asiatic race
ASIATIC	from eastern Europe to the Bering Straits—and beyond
AUSTRALIAN	native peoples of the island continent
EUROPEAN	from the Sahara to the Arctic Ocean, from Iceland to the Caucasus
INDIC	native peoples of the Indian sub-continent
MELANESIAN	native to New Zealand and a band of islands northeast of Australia
MICRONESIAN	native peoples of the Micronesian islands in the South Pacific
POLYNESIAN	from the South Pacific islands between New Zealand and Easter island

only 9

8 insects

Insects, insects everywhere! Around the clock and around the globe:

ANT	a social insect, an endlessly active tunneler and master builder
LUNA MOTH	nocturnal moth of great size and beauty—literally, moon moth
GRASSHOPPER	meadow jumper and flyer
DRAGONFLY	acrobatic mosquito hunter
CICADA	or locust—from a nice hum in the summer trees to a famine-causing horde
LADYBUG	more truly called a ladybird beetle, and not a bug at all
FIREFLY	or lightning bug—a night-flying beetle who heralds the arrival of summer
HONEYBEE	social like the ant, a tireless worker, an amazing geometric nest builder

and many more

7 seas

Saltwater seas, geographically diverse, culturally significant:

MEDITERRANEAN	borders some of the Earth's oldest civilizations
BERING	links Asia and North America and the Pacific and Arctic Oceans
RED	surrounded by deserts rich in history
CARRIBEAN	the tropical sea of the Americas
NORTH	Europe's stormy gateway to the North Atlantic
CORAL	Oceania's tropical sea
SEA OF JAPAN	Japan's gateway to Asia, and vice versa
SOUTH CHINA	some of the busiest, most ancient sea lanes on Earth

and many more

6 mountains   The tallest mountains on the six populated continents:
EVEREST   Asia; tallest on Earth; 29,028 feet
ACONCAGUA   South America's tallest; 22,834 feet
MCKINLEY   North America's tallest; 20,320 feet
KILIMANJARO   Africa's tallest; 19,340
MONT BLANC   Europe's tallest; 15,771 feet
KOSCIUSKO   Australia's tallest; 7,310 feet
and many more

5 lakes   Earth's largest lake is the Caspian Sea, an inland saltwater sea.
SUPERIOR   North America's largest; Earth's second largest; largest body of fresh water
LADOGA   Europe's largest
TANGANYIKA   Africa's largest with an African place name (largest is Lake Victoria)
BAIKAL   Asia's largest freshwater lake, and Earth's deepest—over one mile!
EYRE   Australia's largest, but the smallest on this short list
and many more

4 winds   Named for the points of the compass from which they blow:
NORTH   blows cold in the northern hemisphere, hot in the southern
SOUTH   blows hot in the northern hemisphere, cold in the southern
EAST   in the arctic and tropical climate zones, east winds prevail
WEST   in the temperate climate zone, west winds prevail
only 4

3 rivers   The two longest rivers, and the one where Mark Twain piloted steamboats:
NILE   Africa; 4,160 miles
AMAZON   South America; 4,100 miles
MISSISSIPPI   North America; 2,348 miles (if the Missouri river is added on—4,881 miles!)
and many more

2 hemispheres   Divide Earth at the equator for two more—NORTHERN and SOUTHERN.
EASTERN   in general, the half that contains Europe, Asia, Africa, and Australia
WESTERN   in general, the half that contains North and South America
and 2 more

1 earth   ...and the end.
only 1

SEP 0 6 1995

WEST END

J 510 CLEMENTS   WEST E
Clements, Andrew
Mother Earth's counting
   book

Atlanta-Fulton Public Library

R780120806